RESTLESS PLANET

VOLCANOES

Vincent Bunce

RESTLESS PLANET

VOLCANOES

Other titles in this series:

EARTHQUAKES FLOODS STORMS

Cover photograph: Two scientists brave the lava flow to monitor an erupting volcano on the island of Heimay, near Iceland.

Title page: A vulcanologist at work at Krafla in Iceland.

Contents page: Red hot lava flows into the Pacific Ocean off Hawaii, causing huge explosions of gas and steam.

This book is dedicated to Calum, Dominic, Timothy and Maria.

Consultant: Bill Clarke, Education Officer,
The Natural History Museum
Editor: Alison Cooper
Series editors: Polly Goodman and Philippa Smith
Book design: Tim Mayer

First published in 1999 by Wayland Publishers Ltd
61 Western Road, Hove, East Sussex
BN3 1JD England
www.wayland.co.uk

© Copyright 1999 Wayland Publishers Ltd

British Library Cataloguing in Publication Data
Bunce, Vincent
Volcanoes. – (Restless Planet)
1.Volcanoes – Juvenile literature
I.Title
551.2′1

ISBN 0 7502 2471 1

Printed and bound in Italy by G. Canale & C.S.p.A.

Acknowledgements
The publishers would like to thank the following for allowing their photographs to be reproduced in this book: Bruce Coleman *Contents page*/Pacific Stock, 6/Orion Service & Trading Co Inc., 16/C.C. Lockwood, 19/Pacific Stock, 33/Derek Croucher, 36/Stephen Bond, 40/Dr Sandro Prato; DERA/Still Pictures 32; ET Archive/National Gallery 22; Mary Evans 29; GeoScience Features 7, 21, 42, 43; Michael Holford 28; Image Bank 45 (bottom)/Guido A. Rossi; Impact 24/Andy Johnstone; Michael Holford 28; NASA GSFC/Science Photo Library 21; Oxford Scientific Films 35/Norbert Rosing, 39 (bottom)/Richard Packwood; Photri 37/Mark E. Gibson; Planet Earth *Cover & Title page*/I. & V. Krafft, 11 (top)/Krafft, 14/Annie Price, 15/Krafft, 18/V. & I. Bourseiller, 31/William M. Smithey Jr, 34/Frank Krahmer, 39 (top)/I. & V. Krafft, 41/Annie Price, 44-5/I. & V. Krafft; Popperfoto 27/Colin Braley/Reuters; Frank Spooner/Gamma 4-5/Alain Buu, 20/Bouvet, Hires & Duclos; Wayland Picture Library 5 (top).
Artwork: Peter Bull 8; Nick Hawken 9, 20; Tim Mayer 7, 10, 12, 13, 14, 15, 17, 25, 30, 31, 37, 38; Malcolm Walker 35, 43.

Contents

Introducing Volcanoes

An erupting volcano is one of the most spectacular sights in the world. It is also extremely dangerous. In just a few minutes the huge explosive power of a volcano can eject poisonous gases and millions of tonnes of dust into the earth's atmosphere. It can cover an entire landscape in red-hot lava or ash, killing vegetation and wildlife, destroying settlements and disrupting communications. Some eruptions can also lead to huge loss of life.

▼ The Soufrière Hills volcano in Montserrat made news headlines around the world in 1997. Eruptions devastated the island and two-thirds of the islanders abandoned their homes to live overseas.

◀ Devastation on the island of Martinique, following the 1902 eruption of Mont Pelée.

66 EYEWITNESS 99

"As we approached St Pierre we could distinguish the red flames that belched from the mountain in huge volumes and gushed into the sky. Enormous clouds of black smoke hung over the volcano... There was a constant muffled roar. There was a tremendous explosion about 7.45 a.m., soon after we got in. The mountain was blown to pieces. The side of the volcano was ripped out and a solid wall of flame was hurled straight towards us.

The wave of fire was on us and over us like a flash of lightning. The fire rolled straight down on St Pierre and the ships that were moored there. Wherever the mass of fire struck the sea, the water boiled and sent up vast columns of steam.

Before the volcano burst, the waterside area of St Pierre was crowded with people. After the explosion, not one living soul was seen on the land."

An account of the eruption of Mont Pelée on the island of Martinique in 1902, written by an officer on a ship in the harbour.

What is a volcano ?

A volcano is really just an opening in the earth's surface through which molten rock called magma can escape, often with gas and dust. Usually we only hear about the very powerful eruptions which affect large numbers of people. But at any one time, up to twenty volcanoes may be erupting somewhere in the world. Volcanoes come in different shapes and sizes, and there are several types of eruption. An eruption can be very destructive, killing thousands of people and destroying farmland and settlements. It changes the landscape completely. But an eruption can create new land as well as destroying it.

How many volcanoes are there?

There are about 550 active volcanoes on land. Each year around 50 of these erupt, though only a few eruptions are serious enough to affect people or cause great damage. Not all volcanoes are still active. Some, like Mount Kilimanjaro in Kenya, have not erupted for many thousands of years. These are called extinct volcanoes. Others have remained quiet for a long time. Known as sleeping or dormant volcanoes, they can suddenly come to life and erupt again. One example is Mount Fuji in Japan, which last erupted in 1707.

Apart from the 550 or so active volcanoes on land, there are many more on the floors of our seas and oceans. These bubble away mostly unseen. In fact, over 80 per cent of the earth's surface (above and below sea-level) is actually volcanic in origin. Volcanoes have played a key role in the development of the earth. Not only do they help to create new rock, but gas emissions from the early volcanoes, hundreds of millions of years ago, formed the earth's atmosphere, which in turn provided the conditions which helped life to develop.

 DID YOU KNOW ?

Scientists estimate that about 200,000 people have been killed as a result of volcanic eruptions in the last 500 years. Between 1980 and 1990, volcanic activity led to 26,000 deaths and caused 450,000 people to flee from their homes.

▼ Japan's Mount Fuji is a dormant volcano.

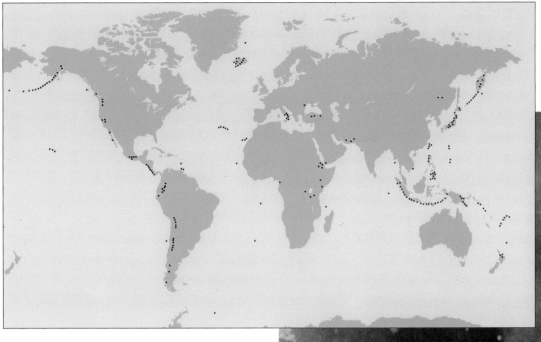

▲ The red dots on this map show the location of volcanoes around the world.

Where are volcanoes found?

Although there are several hundred active volcanoes, they are not distributed evenly around the world. There is a pattern to their location. Most are concentrated around the edges of the continents, as the map above shows. Others form chains of islands, or long, underwater mountain ranges in the oceans. More than half the world's active volcanoes above sea-level circle the Pacific Ocean, and are known as the 'Ring of Fire'.

Jets of water known as 'black smokers' ▶ bubble up from the ocean floor in areas of volcanic activity. These are in the eastern Pacific Ocean.

What Causes Volcanoes?

To understand what causes volcanoes, you need to understand how the earth is made up. The earth has three main layers: the crust, the mantle and the core. The crust is made up of solid rock and varies in thickness. It is more than 60 km thick under mountain chains like the Alps and Himalayas, but just 5 km under the oceans. The mantle is a thick layer of molten rock (called magma), and the core is made up of an outer liquid layer and a solid centre.

Temperatures inside the earth are very high – over 5,000 °C in the core. This means that the planet on which we live is like a huge fiery ball of hot molten rock, surrounded by a few kilometres of relatively cool, hard rock – the crust. Because heat rises, the magma in the earth's mantle has to find a way to rise upwards through the crust above it, rather like the way that hot air rises.

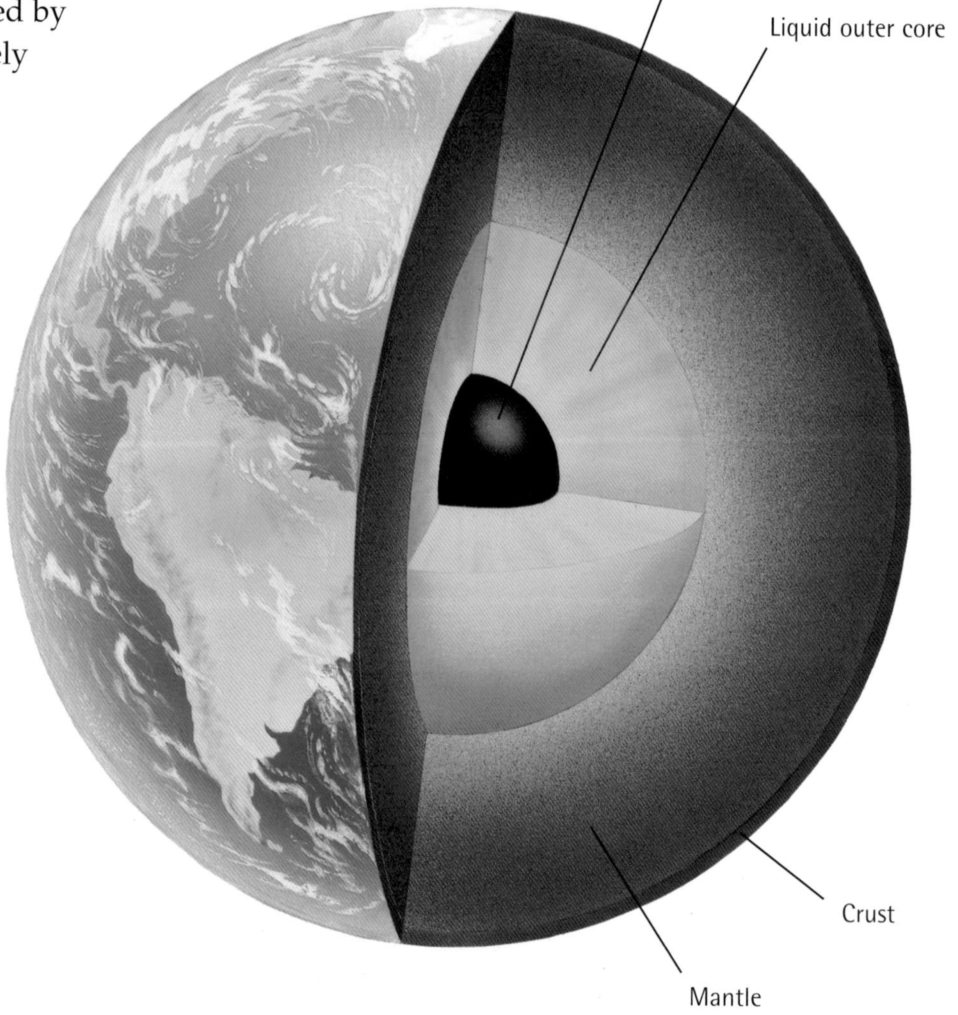

Solid inner core

Liquid outer core

The structure of the earth. ▶ Hot currents of molten rock swirl through the mantle.

Crust

Mantle

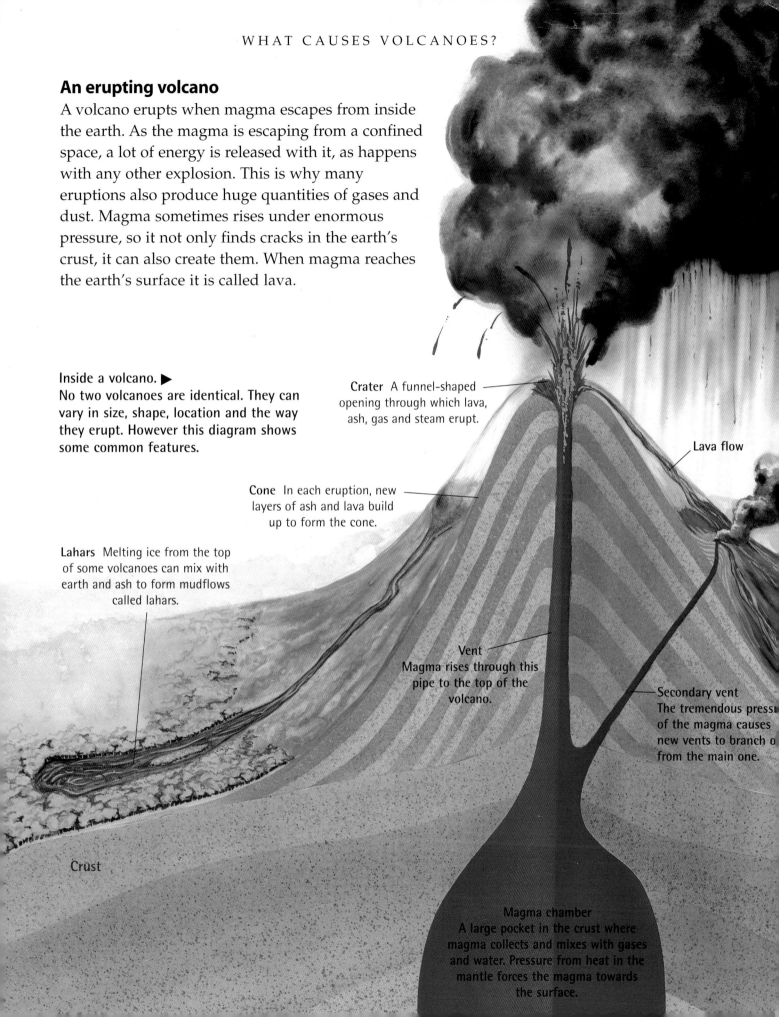

An erupting volcano

A volcano erupts when magma escapes from inside the earth. As the magma is escaping from a confined space, a lot of energy is released with it, as happens with any other explosion. This is why many eruptions also produce huge quantities of gases and dust. Magma sometimes rises under enormous pressure, so it not only finds cracks in the earth's crust, it can also create them. When magma reaches the earth's surface it is called lava.

Inside a volcano. ▶
No two volcanoes are identical. They can vary in size, shape, location and the way they erupt. However this diagram shows some common features.

Crater A funnel-shaped opening through which lava, ash, gas and steam erupt.

Lava flow

Cone In each eruption, new layers of ash and lava build up to form the cone.

Lahars Melting ice from the top of some volcanoes can mix with earth and ash to form mudflows called lahars.

Vent
Magma rises through this pipe to the top of the volcano.

Secondary vent
The tremendous pressu of the magma causes new vents to branch o from the main one.

Crust

Magma chamber
A large pocket in the crust where magma collects and mixes with gases and water. Pressure from heat in the mantle forces the magma towards the surface.

Tectonic plates and volcanoes

The earth's crust is its thinnest layer. It is broken up into large pieces, called tectonic plates. These plates lie above the hot, liquid mantle. Each plate contains some continental crust (land) and some oceanic crust (sea-bed). Huge currents of molten rock circulate deep in the mantle, causing the plates to move about very slowly on the earth's surface.

DID YOU KNOW?

The word 'volcano' comes from a tiny island called Vulcano, which is in the Mediterranean Sea near Sicily. Thousands of years ago, people believed that Vulcano, was the chimney of the forge belonging to Vulcan, the blacksmith to the Roman gods. They believed that the lava and dust erupting from Vulcano came from the blacksmith's forge.

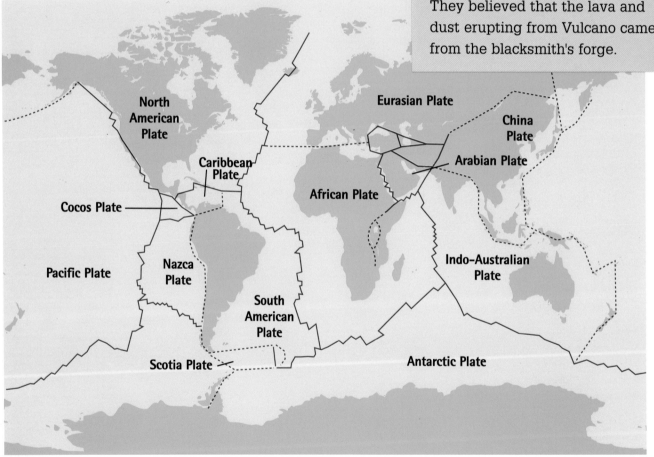

If you look at the location of volcanoes in relation to these plates (see page 7), you will notice some similarities. Many of the world's volcanoes occur along the edges or boundaries of the plates. This is no coincidence. Plate boundaries are among the most geologically active places on earth. Here, new rock is being both created and destroyed, so this is where most of the world's volcanic eruptions and earthquakes occur.

▲ This map shows the boundaries of the earth's tectonic plates. Most volcanic eruptions and earthquakes also occur in these areas.

The Pacific 'Ring of Fire'

More than half of all the world's volcanoes are found in the Pacific 'Ring of Fire'. This area forms a circle stretching down the eastern side of the Pacific Ocean, from Alaska in the north, through the Rocky Mountains of Canada and the USA, to the Andes mountains of South America. It loops back around the western side of the Pacific, up through New Zealand, Indonesia and Japan. Many of the world's most famous volcanoes are found in this 'Ring of Fire': Cotopaxi Ecuador, which last erupted in 1928; Mount St Helens in the USA, which erupted spectacularly in 1980; and Krakatoa in Indonesia, which killed 36,000 people when it erupted in 1883.

Asia

North America

PACIFIC OCEAN

South America

A(

▲ Active volcano
△ Extinct volcano

▲ This map shows the volcanoes that make up the Pacific 'Ring of Fire'.

Spreading centres

Some plate boundaries follow the line of the land surface. For example, the eastern edge of the Pacific Plate seems to run down the coast of the American continent. Others are found at the bottom of the world's oceans. Here, hidden from view, lie extensive ranges of mountains, canyons and volcanoes. New rock is being created here by volcanoes spewing out lava underwater. Scientists estimate that between 2–5 cm of new crust is created each year by volcanoes along the Mid-Atlantic Ocean Ridge.

▼ At almost 5,900 m above sea-level, Cotopaxi volcano in Ecuador is considered to be the world's highest active volcano.

Types of volcano

There are three main types of volcano. Scientists decide what type a volcano is by examining the plate movements that have caused it to form.

1. Subduction volcanoes

Subduction volcanoes occur where plates move towards each other and collide. The areas where this happens are called destructive plate margins, because the earth's crust is being destroyed. The diagrams on this page show the three main types of destructive plate margin, where subduction volcanoes are formed.

One plate, usually the one that is heavier or more dense, is forced to dive (subduct) beneath the other into the mantle, causing it to heat up and melt. This melted material pushes its way back to the earth's surface under great pressure, and often erupts explosively. The area where the two pieces of crust are in contact is called the subduction zone.

These diagrams show how subduction volcanoes form at destructive plate margins.

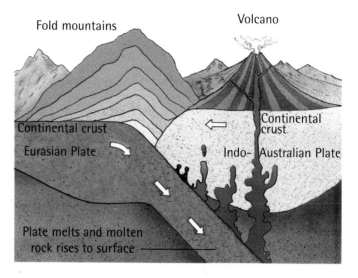

▲ 2. Continent to continent margins

Where two plates carrying continental crust collide, for example where the Indo-Australian Plate meets the Eurasian Plate in northern India, the continental crust crumples to form fold mountains. Here, the melting crust which is forced into the mantle by the collision can again cause volcanic eruptions.

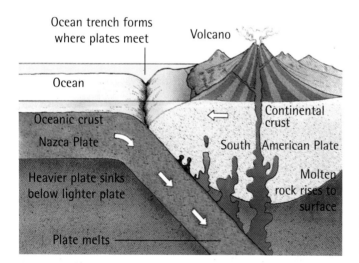

▲ 1. Ocean to continent margins

Along the western coast of South America, a collision zone has formed where the Nazca Plate meets the South American plate. The Nazca Plate sinks below the lighter continental crust of the South American Plate, leading to some violent volcanic eruptions in the Andes.

▲ 3. Ocean to ocean margins

Sometimes, two plates which are made up of oceanic crust meet. Here again one plate subducts. When magma rises to the surface it forms a chain of volcanoes known as an island arc, like the Lesser Antilles in the Eastern Caribbean, and the Aleutians and the islands of Japan in the Pacific Ocean.

2. Rift volcanoes

Where plates are moving apart, as in the middle of the Atlantic Ocean, magma rises through the gap between the separating plates and creates new rock. Here the volcanoes are known as rift volcanoes.

There are more rift volcanoes than subduction volcanoes, but we hear far less about them. Most of them are hidden from view on the ocean floor, and they do not often threaten human life or property. Also, they usually erupt more gently than other types of volcano, with lava that oozes rather than explodes from inside them.

Iceland, which straddles the Mid-Atlantic Ocean Ridge, and the Rift Valley of East Africa are two of the few places where rift volcanoes are found on land.

3. Hot-spot volcanoes

Some volcanoes are found away from the edges of the plates. They are formed where rising plumes of magma force their way to the surface from deep within the mantle – a 'hot spot'. As the plate moves, the existing volcano is carried away from the hot spot and becomes extinct. The next time the pressure builds up, new magma erupts to form another volcano in its place.

The best-known hot-spot volcanoes are in the Hawaiian Islands. The oldest islands in the west, such as Niihau and Kauai, contain extinct volcanoes, but the eastern islands of Maui and Hawaii itself still have active volcanoes.

The formation of rift volcanoes

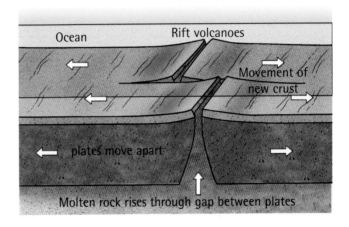

The formation of 'hot-spot' volcanoes

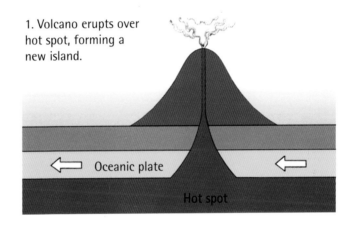

1. Volcano erupts over hot spot, forming a new island.

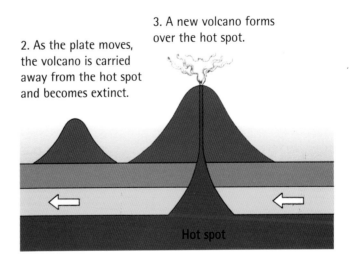

2. As the plate moves, the volcano is carried away from the hot spot and becomes extinct.

3. A new volcano forms over the hot spot.

Volcanic forms

The shape and size of a volcano are determined by:
- the type of eruption
- the type of lava which is produced in the eruption
- the relative amounts of lava and ash which build up to form the volcano.

Volcanoes come in many shapes and sizes but they can be grouped into the four main types described on these two pages.

Ash and cinder cone volcanoes occur where an explosive eruption hurls small, solid fragments of ash and rock from the volcano's vent. The ash and rock build up to form volcanoes that are steep-sided but not very tall. This type of volcano is found in the Craters of the Moon area in Idaho, USA. Another example is Paricutin in Mexico.

Acid lava cone volcanoes are made up of lava which is thick or viscous. This flows very slowly, like treacle, and does not extend very far from the vent. It forms cones that have steep sides. An example is Mount Ngauruhoe in New Zealand which last erupted in 1975.

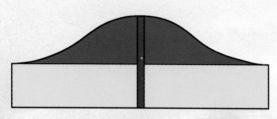

▲ An ash and cinder cone volcano

▲ An acid lava cone volcano

▼ Mount Ngauruhoe in New Zealand is an acid lava cone volcano.

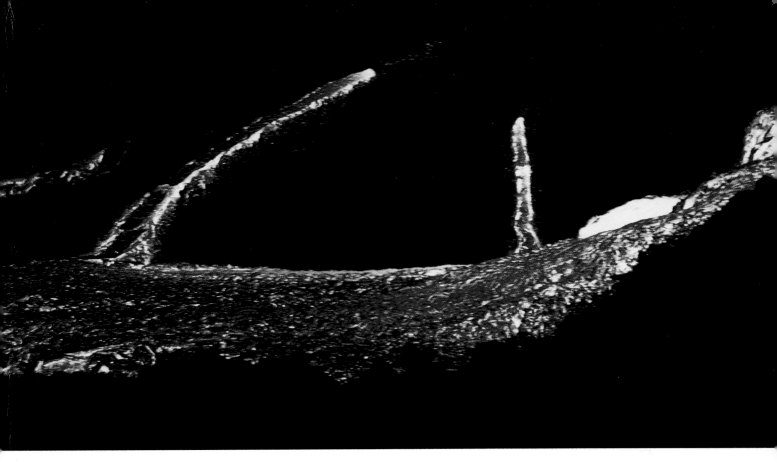

▲ The lava that flows from Piton de la Fournaise, on Réunion Island, has created a shield volcano. Piton de la Fournaise is one of the most active volcanoes on earth, and has erupted more than 150 times since 1640.

Shield volcanoes, like Mauna Loa on Hawaii in the Pacific Ocean, and Piton de la Fournaise on Réunion Island in the Indian Ocean, are made up of basalt-rich lava which is thin, runny and spreads a long way from the vent. As a result, shield volcanoes are very large but have very gently sloping sides. Shield volcanoes are mostly made up of lava and contain very little ash or cinder (approximately 95 per cent lava and 5 per cent ash).

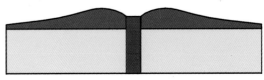

▲ A shield volcano

Composite cone volcanoes, also known as **stratovolcanoes,** make up more than 60 per cent of all volcanoes on earth. They are usually quite tall. They are formed by a cycle of quiet eruptions of runny lava followed by explosive eruptions of thick lava. Stratovolcanoes have more ash than shield volcanoes. This combination of high ash content and a thick, slow-moving lava means that their sides are much steeper than shield volcanoes. Mount St Helens in the USA, Pinatubo in the Philippines and Fuji in Japan are all examples of composite cone volcanoes.

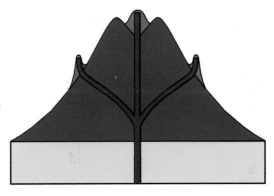

▲ A composite cone volcano

Volcanic eruptions

The exact nature of a volcanic eruption is related to the type of lava which spills out on to the earth's surface. Some lava is thin and runny, and flows freely. Eruptions of this type of lava are usually fairly gentle. Thicker lava tends to erupt much more explosively. It cools quickly too, and may form a solid plug inside the main vent of a volcano.

Calderas

If the vent of a volcano is blocked, pressure builds up below the blockage. Eventually the pressure may become so great that there is an explosion which blows off the top of the volcano. This creates a large crater at the top called a caldera. Over a long period of time, if the volcano remains inactive, the crater can fill with water, creating a crater lake. Calderas are often more than 5 km in diameter. The world's largest caldera is at Mount Aso on Kyushu, the most southern of Japan's four main islands. It is 22 km long and about 16 km wide.

▼ This is Crater Lake at the top of Mount Mazama in Oregon, USA.

Types of volcanic eruption

Volcanoes can be divided according to the explosiveness of their eruptions, as the illustrations on the right show. The least severe are known as Hawaiian eruptions – these generally produce shield volcanoes. The most severe are called Plinian eruptions – these often involve the collapse of the volcano's cone and the formation of a caldera. Plinian eruptions were named after the Roman scholar Pliny the Elder, who lost his life, when Mount Vesuvius erupted in AD 79. His nephew, Pliny the Younger, wrote to Tacitus describing the eruption as it began.

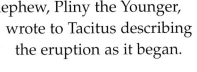

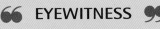

66 EYEWITNESS 99

"On Mount Vesuvius, wide leaping sheets of flame blazed from several places, a brilliant glare against the night's darkness. There had been earth tremors for several days, but that night they became so strong that everything seemed to be turned upside down . . . Then we saw the sea sucked back into itself as though driven by the earth's tremors. Many sea creatures were left scattered over the dry sands of the exposed shoreline. In the other direction a terrifying black cloud was riven by bursts of twisted, flickering fire and elongated tongues of flame. They were like flashes of lightning but much larger . . . Ashes were already falling. Behind, a dense black cloud was threatening, following us like floodwater spreading over the earth . . . Many raised their hands in prayer to the gods, but many more believed there were no more gods and that the world was lost in eternal night."

An extract from Pliny the Younger's letter to Cornelius Tacitus, a Roman senator and historian, describing the eruption of Vesuvius in AD 79.

Hawaiian ▶
The least violent type of eruption. Large amounts of runny lava erupt and produce large volcanoes with gentle slopes.

Strombolian ▶
Mild but fairly regular eruptions. Small sticky lava bombs, ash, gas and glowing cinders erupt.

◀ Vulcanian
Violent eruptions shoot out very thick lava and large lava bombs.

▼ Peléean
A violent type of eruption. Thick, sticky lava is accompanied by a burning cloud of ash, gas and pumice (a *nuée ardente*, which is French for 'fiery cloud').

Plinian ▶
The most violent type of eruption. Cinders, gas and ash are flung explosively high into the air. The volcano cone often collapses to form a caldera.

Volcanic Hazards

Think of a volcano erupting. What comes into your mind? A spectacular torrent of red-hot lava, engulfing all in its path? In reality lava flows are only one of many volcanic hazards, and among the least harmful. The wide variety of hazards which affect both people and the landscape can be divided into direct (primary) and indirect (secondary) hazards.

Primary hazards

The direct hazards of volcanic activity are ash, dust, lava and poisonous gases.

Ash and dust

The explosive power of a volcanic eruption causes old lava to be blasted into tiny pieces and hurled into the air, sometimes several kilometres high, with ash and dust. The size of this material ranges from fine ash and dust particles, to pebble-sized rock fragments and volcanic bombs of molten lava, measuring 25 cm or more across, that solidify as they fly through the air. These airborne fragments are known as tephra.

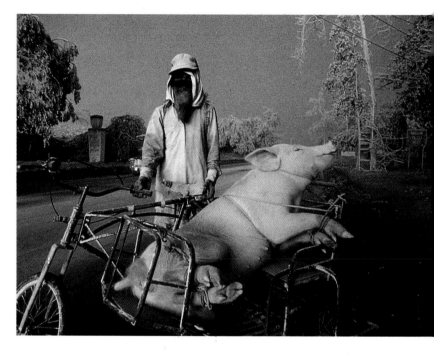

▲ Heavy ash falls followed the eruption of Mount Pinatubo in the Philippines in 1991. Here, a farmer tries to move his pig to safety.

▼ This diagram shows the different types of volcanic hazards.

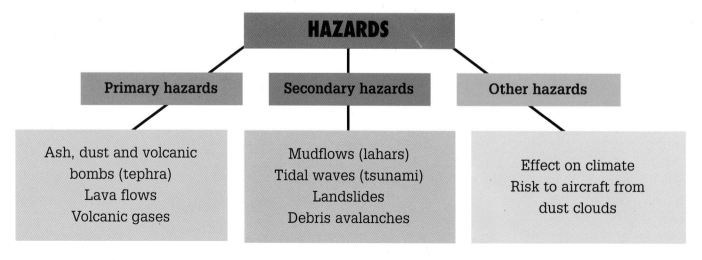

HAZARDS		
Primary hazards	Secondary hazards	Other hazards
Ash, dust and volcanic bombs (tephra) Lava flows Volcanic gases	Mudflows (lahars) Tidal waves (tsunami) Landslides Debris avalanches	Effect on climate Risk to aircraft from dust clouds

Often, tephra is spread over a wide area. Heavy tephra falls can damage buildings, causing roofs to collapse. Ash and dust hang in the air, making it difficult for people to breathe and for machinery to work. When the ash falls to the ground vast areas of fertile agricultural land may be smothered. When Vesuvius erupted in AD 79, the city of Pompeii was buried under 6 m of ash.

Sometimes, instead of being blasted upwards, hot ash clouds flow down the sides of a volcano like an avalanche, reaching speeds of up to 300 kph and burning everything in their path. These are called *nuée ardentes*.

Lava

Lava does not often threaten people's lives because it moves slowly, perhaps only a few centimetres per hour. Occasionally though, basaltic lava can flow much more quickly. Around 300 people were killed by lava travelling at more than 30 kph when Mount Nyiragongo in Zaire erupted in 1986.

Volcanic gases

Magma contains dissolved gases, such as water vapour, carbon monoxide and sulphur oxides. When volcanoes erupt, these foul-smelling gases are released into the atmosphere. Popocatépetl near Mexico City, has erupted more than 17 times in the last 50 years. Geologists estimate that 'El Popo' releases 8,000 tonnes of sulphur dioxide gas into the atmosphere each day.

▲ Red hot lava flows into the Pacific Ocean off Hawaii causing huge explosions of gas and steam.

CAMEROON VOLCANO: DANGER AREAS TO BE EVACUATED

Villages in the central African state of Cameroon are to be evacuated on Monday as lava flows from Mount Cameroon threaten homes and businesses. The 4,100-m volcano in the south-west of the country began erupting last week for the first time since 1982. Gas masks have been issued to people living in the area to protect them from dust and dangerous gases. President Biya flew in by helicopter yesterday to inspect the damage.

Adapted from Reuters reports, April 1999

Secondary hazards

Volcanic eruptions can lead to less direct hazards, sometimes known as secondary hazards. These include lahars (mudflows), avalanches and tsunami (tidal waves).

Lahars

As ash and dust move down the sides of a volcano, they may mix with water from a crater lake, or from rivers, to form a mudflow. This will often contain rocks of different sizes and will gather power as it moves downhill. Lahars can vary in width from just a few centimetres to several hundred metres, and can travel distances of up to 300 km.

The 1985 Nevado del Ruiz eruption in western Colombia, South America, took place high in the Andes mountains. A cloud of hot gas from the volcano melted the snow cap and nearby glaciers, releasing huge quantities of water. This, combined with ash and rock debris from the eruption, formed a lahar that was 40 m deep. It rushed downhill at speeds of up to 50 kph, engulfing the town of Armero, 50 km away, in over 8 m of mud. More than 22,000 people lost their lives.

▲ A survivor of the lahar that swept through Armero in 1985 sits among the wreckage.

▼ This diagram shows how the town of Armero was buried by a lahar following the 1985 Nevado del Ruiz eruption.

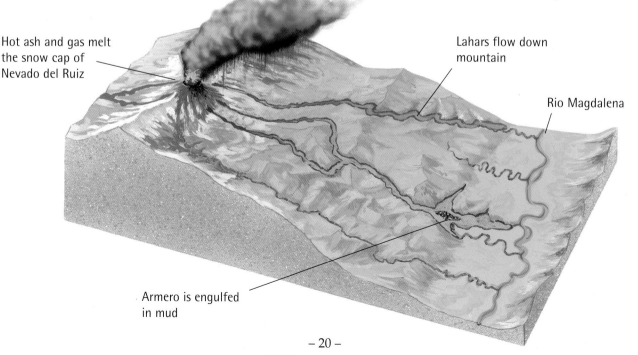

Hot ash and gas melt the snow cap of Nevado del Ruiz

Lahars flow down mountain

Rio Magdalena

Armero is engulfed in mud

Landslides and debris avalanches

Volcanic eruptions are often accompanied by earth tremors or small earthquakes. These can set off landslides or avalanches of loose rock and volcanic material. This is exactly what happened when one side of the USA's Mount St Helens volcano collapsed during its May 1980 eruption.

Tsunami

Some large eruptions generate huge tidal waves called tsunami, which travel at great speed. One such tsunami was triggered by the Krakatoa eruption of 1883. This produced 30-m-high waves which devastated the coastlines of many neighbouring islands, drowning more than 36,000 people. It is not only land-based volcanoes that can set off tidal waves. Underwater eruptions, which release large volumes of gas into the oceans, can stir up the water above them, creating huge tidal waves which may cause flooding.

▼ An avalanche of rock cascades down the slopes of Mount St Helens as the side of the volcano is blown out by the eruption.

Wider-scale effects

Apart from the effects on the immediate area around a volcano, an eruption can have other consequences, far away from the volcano itself.

Records indicate that blackened skies and fiery sunsets are often seen in the immediate aftermath of an eruption. They are caused when dust from the volcano hangs in the air. Effects such as these can be seen far from the original blast, and may go beyond simply changing the colour of the skies. Some scientists believe that the dinosaurs died out on earth when a dust cloud resulting from a series of huge volcanic eruptions blocked out the sun. The lack of sunlight and cooler temperatures which resulted from this meant that many plants died. The plant-eating dinosaurs soon died out too and the dinosaurs that fed on them could no longer survive.

▼ *The Fighting Temeraire* by the English artist J.M.W. Turner. The striking, colourful skies that appear in many of his paintings may have been inspired by the dust-filled sunsets which followed the massive eruption of Tambora in Indonesia in 1815.

Spreading dust clouds

The precise effects of volcanoes on our climate are still uncertain. The ash and dust cloud from the eruption of Tambora in Indonesia, in 1815, led to a fall in world temperatures of 1.1 °C. There was a reddish-yellow haze in skies all over Europe in the months after the eruption. The following year was known as 'the year without a summer'. Food crops were damaged in parts of Europe, and heavy unseasonal snowfalls fell in much of the north-eastern USA.

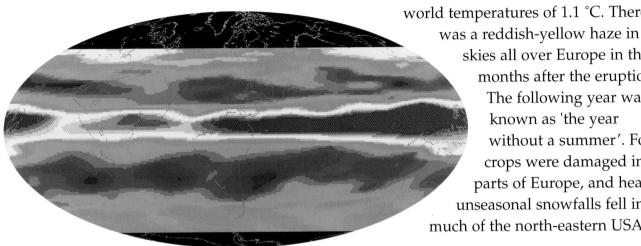

▲ This satellite image was recorded in 1986, following the eruption of Mount Louise in northern South America. The red band around the Equator indicates high levels of ash and dust in the atmosphere in this area.

If volcanic dust clouds are blasted high enough into the atmosphere by the power of an eruption, winds blow them great distances around the globe. Evidence of this comes from satellites. In 1991, dust clouds thrown 40 km into the atmosphere from Mount Pinatubo in the Philippines travelled around the world in under four weeks. Scientists calculated that 2 per cent of the incoming sunlight was deflected by this dust cloud, causing slightly lower temperatures worldwide. In the longer term, volcanic dust is believed to remain in the atmosphere for several years.

Aircraft flying near an eruption may experience problems caused by ash and dust. This happened to a KLM jet with 248 people on board in 1990, when it flew close to the erupting Redoubt volcano in Alaska, USA. Ash from the volcano stalled all four engines, and the plane tumbled more than 3,900 m before the pilot regained control and landed safely at Anchorage.

ALASKA VOLCANO THREATENS AIRCRAFT

A pilot flying high above Alaska's Aleutian Islands was one of the first to spot the latest eruption of the Shishaldin volcano, say seismologists at the Alaska Volcano Observatory. Following two months of rumbling, a cloud of ash and steam erupted from the volcano and rose 9 km into the atmosphere. The eruption is considered to pose a threat to aircraft in the area and scheduled flights to Unalaska/Dutch Harbor have been cancelled.

Adapted from Reuters report, April 20 1999

Volcanic Disasters

Montserrat

In July 1995, people living on the tiny island of Montserrat in the Caribbean awoke one morning and noticed a sulphurous smell in the air. No one knew where it was coming from until experts traced it to a spot not far from the main cone of the Chances Peak volcano, in the south of the island. There had been no major eruptions from this volcano for 400 year, but now it was coming to life again.

Why did the volcano erupt ?

Volcanic activity in Montserrat occurs because two tectonic plates meet about 300 km north-east of the island. Here, the North American Plate meets the Caribbean Plate and, because it is more dense, is forced below the Caribbean Plate. As it descends into the mantle it melts. Then the molten magma forces its way up through the crust, finding its way explosively to the surface at Chances Peak.

▲ A cloud of ash and dust pours from the Chances Peak volcano in 1995.

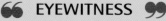 EYEWITNESS

"People became concerned and those living nearby were moved to a safer part of the island. Then the volcano stem began to grow. There were mudflows and steam, and veins began to open up in the side of the volcano."

Doris Francis, a local schoolteacher (quoted in the Newcastle Journal, November 1997)

Montserrat volcano diary

1995

18 July Small earthquakes, tephra falls and steam explosions suggest a major eruption is imminent.

Mid-August 6,000 people are evacuated to the northern end of the island.

21 August Largest eruption to date. Ash and dust fall on Plymouth, the capital, causing 30 minutes of darkness.

December Plymouth is evacuated for the first time. There are several minor ash eruptions.

1996

April More severe eruptions occur. Very hot gas, ash, rock and dust are thrown up to 12 km into the air before flowing down the mountain (this is called a pyroclastic flow). Danger areas are evacuated again.

1997

January Ash and grit fall over most of the island. Major damage to land and property. Pyroclastic flows sweep down the sides of the volcano at up to 200 kph.

25 June Collapse of volcano's dome. Pyroclastic flows cover almost 4 square km. An ash plume reaches 9 km into the air, blocking the sun for 20 minutes.

27 June The first confirmed deaths since the eruptions began are announced. Four people have been buried by debris.

August Plymouth is destroyed by further ash and dust falls, and pyroclastic flows. Ash falls are reported up to 40 km away, on the island of Antigua.

1998 Volcanic activity continues throughout the year...

1999

13 January An eruption sends an avalanche of hot gases and rocks down the eastern side of the volcano and a plume of ash is thrown 6 km into the air.

Montserrat

▼ The island was split into a number of zones, with people allowed to remain in the safer areas.

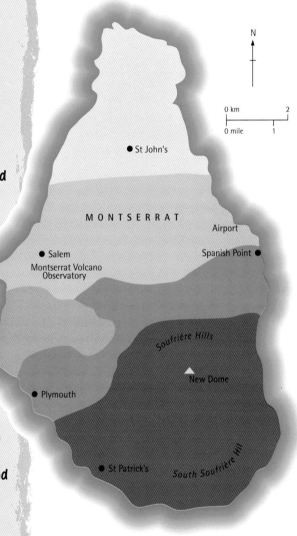

N

0 km 2
0 mile 1

St John's

MONTSERRAT

Airport

Salem
Montserrat Volcano Observatory

Spanish Point

Soufrière Hills

New Dome

Plymouth

St Patrick's

South Soufrière Hill

Hazard zones (April 1997)

No access

Limited access for essential visitors

Prepare for possible evacuation

Full occupation (possible evacuation)

Full occupation

ISLAND CAPITAL THREATENED BY VOLCANO IS EVACUATED

PARTS of the British island of Montserrat were ordered yesterday to be evacuated at night as the threat of a volcanic eruption rose to "red alert".

The Governor of the Caribbean colony, Frank Savage, said people on the south coast, which includes the capital, Plymouth, should move to the north by 6 pm.

They could return to work during the day, he added.

The move followed an eruption of ash from... the Chance's Peak volcano in the Soufrière Hills on Monday afternoon... In a series of emergency radio broadcasts, Mr Savage and his Chief Minister, Reuben Meade, instituted the first stage of evacuation...

About 5,000 residents..., about half the total population, were ordered to move into the northern third of the island, considered safe from the volcano.

The island was reported to be calm, with much of the evacuated population returning yesterday to help clean up the volcanic dust.

An extract from the *Daily Telegraph*, 23 August 1995

Impact of the Soufrière Hills eruption

The island of Montserrat has been seriously affected by over four years of volcanic activity. Twenty people have lost their lives. The southern two-thirds of the island is now totally uninhabitable and is completely deserted. Many of the residents who once lived there have been evacuated or, like schoolteacher Doris Francis, have decided to leave the island. The capital, Plymouth, and the island's only airport have both been abandoned. Seven villages have been entirely destroyed, and there has been widespread damage to property. In just three years, the island's population has been reduced from more than 11,000 to just 4,000.

▲ Newspapers were full of details about the eruption and the plans to evacuate the island.

66 EYEWITNESS 99

"In August 1995, we moved to a safe zone in the north. We returned home weeks later but were moved back to the safe zone in December, where we settled for a few months. I started teaching in a makeshift classroom – a tent. But in June 1997 the volcano burst into life again, producing a huge lava flow. Island life was brought to a standstill. Volcanic ash covered the town of Plymouth (once the capital). We decided it was time to leave."

Doris Francis left the home she shared in Montserrat with her mother and disabled brother in November 1997. Now they live in the north of England. (From *Newcastle Journal*, Nov. 1997)

Helping the victims

Although the future seems uncertain, huge efforts have gone into helping those trying to cope with the disaster. Since Montserrat is an overseas territory of Britain, the British government has played a leading role. By 1998 it had given £59 million in aid. Temporary shelters were made available to house people who had lost their homes. Those wanting to leave Montserrat for nearby islands like Antigua, or to emigrate to Britain, were told that they would be given cash grants.

In 1995, the Montserrat Volcano Observatory was established near Salem, about 6 km from the volcano. Helicopters fly over the volcano daily. The situation is constantly monitored so that people still on the island will have advance warning of future eruptions.

▼ Montserrat's capital, Plymouth, was buried under ash and dust from the volcano and was abandoned.

Major eruptions in history

The Soufrière Hills eruption in Montserrat is just one of the most recent eruptions to make headlines around the world. The eruptions we hear about on television and in the newspapers are usually the most powerful, or those that affect the most people. Some historical eruptions were so devastating that they are still famous today.

Vesuvius, Italy

Perhaps the most famous eruption of all time was in AD 79, when Mount Vesuvius, overlooking the Bay of Naples, suddenly erupted after being dormant for several centuries. A massive explosion blew away the entire top of the mountain, creating a huge cloud of hot ash and gas which was blown south-eastwards towards the towns of Pompeii and Herculaneum. Huge quantities of ash fell on the towns for more than 48 hours. Both towns were buried to a depth of 6 m. When rain fell, the ash turned to concrete, preserving the town exactly as it was when the disaster struck. In the seventeenth century, archaeologists began to uncover the remains.

◄ These ruined buildings are the remains of the Roman town of Pompeii. Vesuvius can be seen in the distance.

Major volcanic eruptions

Yellowstone, USA	2.2 million years BC	2,500 cubic km ash produced
Santorini, Greece	1550 BC	Island destroyed
Vesuvius, Italy	AD 79	Approx. 20,000 dead and town of Pompeii buried under ash
Etna, Italy	1669	20,000 dead
Tambora, Indonesia	1815	92,000 dead
Krakatoa, Indonesia	1883	36,000 dead
Mont Pelée, Martinique	1902	26,000 dead
Novarupta, Alaska, USA	1912	20 cubic km material erupted
Mount St Helens, USA	1980	66 dead
Nevado del Ruiz, Columbia	1984	22,000 dead
Mount Pinatubo, Philippines	1991	420 dead

Krakatoa, Indonesia

In May 1883, a volcano on the Indonesian island of Krakatoa burst into life, sending ash, volcanic gases and pumice into the air. Three months later, on 27 August, there were four giant explosions, the third of which was one of the loudest ever recorded. It was said to have been heard 4,000 km away. The explosion blew the tiny island apart, as the volcano collapsed in on itself.

Ash and dust clouds from this blast rose 80 km into the air, and tidal waves up to 36 m high were produced. The dust cloud circled the earth in under two weeks, causing red sunsets for over a year. The blast was estimated to have been the equivalent of that produced by 200 megatonnes of dynamite. Hundreds of villages along the coastlines of the nearby islands of Java and Sumatra were flooded, with 36,000 lives lost.

▲ This nineteenth-century engraving shows a ship sailing through a sea full of bodies near Krakatoa, on the day after the eruption.

Mount St Helens

In the last thirty years, perhaps the best-known eruption is that of Mount St Helens in the western USA. Mount St Helens is in the Cascade Mountains, and until 18 May 1980, was the fifth-highest mountain in Washington State.

In early May, following minor earth tremors in the area, part of the summit of Mount St Helens bulged outwards visibly. Then, at 8.32 a.m. on 18 May 1980, a violent explosion broke loose a large part of the northern side of the mountain.

A hot, thick cloud of ash and gas slid down the mountainside, incinerating everything in its path. The temperature of the cloud was 260 °C. Trees up to 28 km away were charred by the heat from the blast and 66 people were killed.

The explosion was followed by nine hours of volcanic activity. About 540 million tonnes of ash fell over an area of more than 57,000 square km. Just three days later, air pollution monitoring systems had detected ash from Mount St Helens in the air of cities on the east coast of the USA, some 4,000 km away.

DID YOU KNOW?

The largest eruption in the twentieth century was at Novarupta in Alaska in 1912. Over 20 cubic km of magma explosively erupted in just five days – 30 times the volume erupted by Mount St Helens in 1980.

▼ This diagram shows the causes of the Mount St Helens eruption.

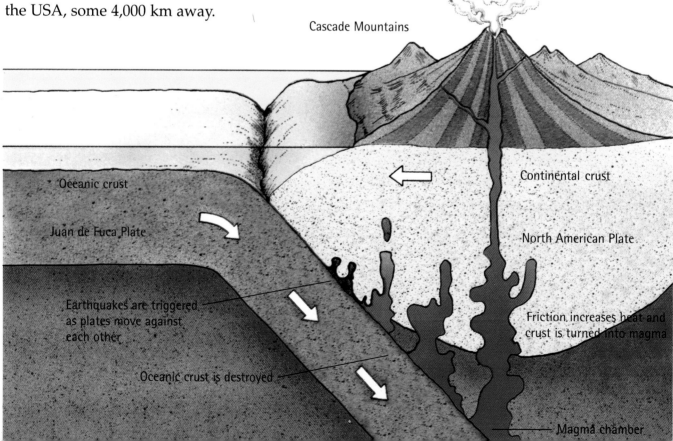

Mount St Helens

Cascade Mountains

Oceanic crust

Juan de Fuca Plate

Earthquakes are triggered as plates move against each other

Oceanic crust is destroyed

Continental crust

North American Plate

Friction increases heat and crust is turned into magma

Magma chamber

▼ The Mount St Helens eruption caused huge damage over a wide area.

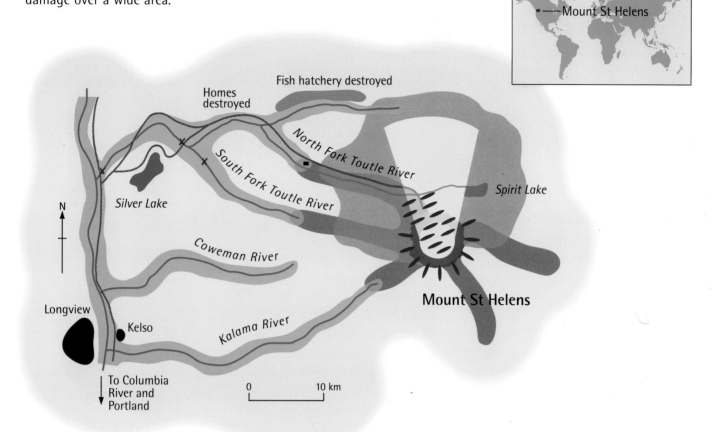

Mount St Helens

Fish hatchery destroyed

Homes destroyed

North Fork Toutle River

South Fork Toutle River

Spirit Lake

N

Silver Lake

Coweman River

Mount St Helens

Longview

Kelso

Kalama River

To Columbia River and Portland

0   10 km

KEY

Blast wave

Landslides and mudflows

Zone of total destruction

Flooded areas

Towns

Main roads

✗   Bridge destroyed

Volcanic bombs and ash

The cone of Mount St Helens ▶ was blown apart in the eruption. Trees destroyed by the blast can be seen at the bottom of the photograph.

Volcanic Landscapes

Volcanic eruptions have the power to completely alter the landscape in just a few seconds. An erupting volcano is capable of destroying settlements, wiping out vegetation, diverting river courses and creating entirely new land surfaces from hardening lava flows, landslides and rock avalanches.

Igneous rocks

Much of the earth's crust is igneous or 'fire-formed'. Extrusive igneous rocks are formed from molten material, such as lava flows, which cools and hardens on the earth's surface. Material that forms from cooling molten magma below the earth's surface is called intrusive (or plutonic) igneous rock.

▲ You can clearly see the Vesuvius volcano, in Italy, on this satellite photograph. It stands out from the surrounding landscape.

There are many different types of igneous rock. Dark, runny lava hardens into a rock called basalt. Because this type of lava moves quickly, it flows over large areas very rapidly, cooling to form basalt plateaus. Basalt is the most common volcanic rock. Thicker lavas flow more slowly, and can form pumice, or a light-coloured rock called rhyolite, or a volcanic glass called obsidian. Granite is the best example of an igneous rock that forms below the earth's surface. It is formed from thick, acidic magma and is found in mountainous areas.

The hexagonal basalt columns of the ▶ Giants Causeway, in Northern Ireland, were formed when a lava flow cooled quickly some 12 million years ago.

Other volcanic landforms

As well as forming volcanoes, red-hot magma within the earth's crust can create other landforms, such as hot springs and geysers. These are formed when magma deep within the mantle heats underground water.

Hot springs

Hot springs occur in many places around the world. They are found where hot magma has worked its way quite close to the earth's surface. Rainwater filtering downwards through the rocks comes into contact with this magma, is heated by it, and then bubbles back towards the surface as a hot spring. The active volcanic areas of Iceland, Japan and New Zealand have large numbers of hot springs. They are also found in older, dormant volcanic areas, such as the Yellowstone National Park in Wyoming and the Snake River Plateau in Idaho, both in the USA.

▲ Hot springs, like these at Lake Bogoria in Kenya, are found in volcanically active areas.

Depth
in metres

Jet of steam and hot water escapes

0

110
120
130
130
130
130

30
60
90
120

Water slowly drips down through the rocks and collects in caverns

Water is superheated to over 300 °C through contact with magma

Temperature °C

Magma

▲ This diagram shows the formation of a geyser.

Geysers

Sometimes underground water is heated so intensely that steam is produced. Water that is under pressure, very deep underground, can be 'superheated' to temperatures in excess of 300 °C. As this superheated water turns into steam it expands explosively. When it reaches the surface, there is a violent eruption – a jet of hot air and steam shoots into the air, often to a great height. This is called a geyser. Once the eruption is over, the geyser refills with water and the process begins again.

Geysers are usually found in areas which are still volcanically active. Iceland has about 30 active geysers. There are more than 100 geysers, many of them quite small, on Russia's Kamchatka Peninsula. However, by far the largest number, about 200 in total, are to be found in Yellowstone National Park in Wyoming, USA.

▼ The Castle Geyser in Yellowstone National Park, USA.

Some geysers erupt at regular intervals: for example 'Old Faithful', a famous geyser in Yellowstone National Park, bursts into life every 30–90 minutes. The largest active geyser in the world is Steamboat Geyser, which is also in Yellowstone National Park. It erupts spectacularly but irregularly, sending steam and water more than 90 m into the air.

Underground activity

Most magma actually hardens while it is still underground, perhaps when it becomes trapped before reaching the surface. The many different landforms that are made by the cooling magma are known as intrusive landforms. They can only be seen if the rock above them is eroded away, or is removed by a volcanic eruption or earthquake.

Batholiths

Batholiths are large, irregular masses of molten rock which solidify within the crust. They usually have a surface area of more than 100 square km. One of the largest batholiths in North America is the Coast Range batholith in Alaska and western Canada, which covers an area of 180,000 square km. In the UK, one of the largest granite batholiths is Dartmoor in south-west England. Much of it is now visible, because the rocks above it have been worn away.

▼ Volcanic rocks that were once underground are now exposed here at Combestone Tor, on Dartmoor in England.

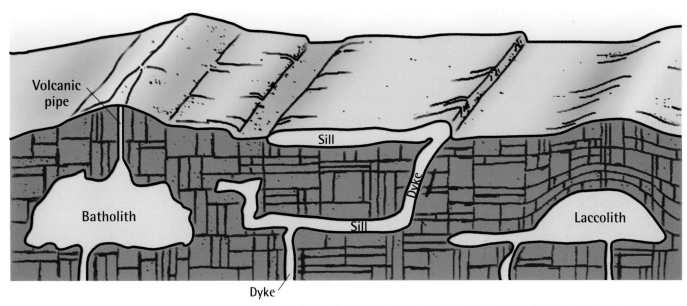

▲ This diagram shows the different types of intrusive landform.

Laccoliths, dykes and sills

Laccoliths are formed when magma forces layers of rock to fold upwards, creating a dome shape. Dykes occur when magma is under so much pressure that it is able to force its way through layers of rock. If a dyke reaches the earth's surface, it is known as a volcanic pipe. Sills form when magma oozes between layers of rock. Both dykes and sills are quite narrow.

Big Bend National Park

Big Bend National Park in south-western Texas, USA, contains some amazing igneous scenery. Volcanic activity between 25 and 70 million years ago resulted in huge quantities of magma solidifying beneath the earth's surface. Nugent Mountain and the Grapevine Hills are examples of huge granite landforms which are visible now that the overlying rock has eroded away.

▼ Mule Ears Peaks is a well-known landform in Big Bend National Park, USA. These peaks are actually two dykes which run parallel to each other.

DID YOU KNOW?

Hekla's lava fields resemble the moon's surface, so US astronauts did some of their training there.

Iceland

Iceland: a volcanic laboratory

Iceland, an island in the North Atlantic, occupies a unique position on the boundary between two continental plates. It sits astride the Mid-Atlantic Ocean Ridge which separates the Eurasian plate from the North American plate. Here, new rock is being created as magma is forced up between the plates. Because of this, Iceland's land area is expanding.

Geologically, Iceland is a young country, with half its land area less than 20 million years old. The entire landscape is covered by evidence of volcanic activity – there are volcanoes, lava fields, hot springs and geysers, as well as newly-formed volcanic islands. The lava fields cover 11 per cent of the land surface. There are more than 200 volcanoes, the most famous being Hekla. This has erupted more than 20 times this century, most recently in 1991.

In November 1996, a volcanic eruption occurred underneath the huge Vatnajökull ice sheet. This led to widespread flooding which destroyed roads and washed bridges away.

New land

Geologists are fascinated by Iceland. Most interest is centred on the huge valley at Thingvellir, east of Reykjavik, in the most volcanically active area. Here, the new rock is actually slowly forcing the North American and Eurasian plates apart.

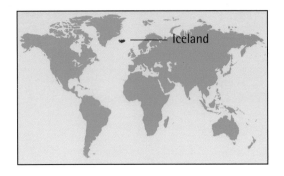

0 km   100
0 mile   60

Mid-Atlantic Ridge

Krafla caldera and power station

Lake Myvatn

ICELAND

Askja

Thingvellir   Geysir
Gullfoss

Reykjavik

1996 eruption   Vatnajökull icecap

Hekla

Heimaey
Westmann Islands
Surtsey   New volcanic zone

N

KEY

Belt of recent volcanic activity

Ice caps

 Volcanoes

▲ In Iceland, volcanic activity is a sign that new land is constantly being created.

▲ A dramatic eruption on the island of Heimaey, just south of Iceland, in 1973.

▼ Swimmers enjoy the natural hot water of Iceland's Blue Lagoon. The power station in the background uses the hot water to supply energy to homes.

On 14 November 1963, a new island called Surtsey was born. It was the ship's cook on a small fishing boat who first noticed black clouds rising from the sea near Iceland's southern coast. Within 24 hours, a new island had been formed. Today it covers an area of over 2.6 square km.

Ten years later, a similar event occurred on the nearby island of Heimaey. This time, activity started around Helgafell, a volcano which had been dormant for 5,000 years. Ash and cinders shot more than 100 m into the air, and lava flowed across the land and into the sea, creating new land and making the island bigger.

Although volcanic activity is hazardous, it brings some benefits. Homes in Reykjavik and many other towns are heated by power which is obtained from the hot springs. The same source is supplying energy to greenhouses where tropical fruits are grown.

Benefits of Volcanoes

Despite the fact that volcanoes can cause great damage to land and property when they erupt, and may even lead to loss of life, more than 350 million people around the world choose to live on or near active volcanoes. In Mexico, 30 million people live within sight of Popocatépetl. In southern Italy, near Naples, 1.5 million people live on the slopes around Mount Vesuvius, still a very active volcano. Why do people take such risks? It is mainly because volcanic activity does have some benefits.

▼ Rice is grown on the rich volcanic soils of Luzon in the Philippines.

Fertile farmland

Over thousands of years, the lava that is spewed out during violent eruptions breaks down slowly to form very fertile soil, which can be successfully used for farming. Hawaii's pineapple and sugar plantations are found on volcanic soils. Some of the best rice-growing areas of Indonesia lie in the shadow of volcanoes. So too do the rich farming lands around Mount Vesuvius in Italy, where olives, vines, nuts and fruit – especially orange and lemon trees – are grown. Elsewhere in this area, further away from the volcano, the land is too barren to grow crops successfully.

▼ A geothermal power station at Taupo in New Zealand.

Volcanic products

The volcanic ash produced by some eruptions is deposited over vast areas. In the short term this ash can be harmful to the environment. But over many years the ash slowly releases valuable nutrients, and if combined with water, it can make the soil more fertile.

The products of volcanoes can be useful in other ways, too. Hot magma, circulating near the earth's surface, heats the rock in contact with it and often turns underground water into superheated steam. The steam can be converted into electricity in special power stations. This type of energy, which is called geothermal energy, is important in parts of Japan, the Philippines, Indonesia and Italy. Elsewhere, metals such as copper, lead, silicon and zinc can be mined from the volcanic rocks found deep underground. Other minerals and some gemstones, such as diamonds and opals, are also concentrated in the igneous rock produced by volcanoes.

Predicting Eruptions

Scientists now understand why volcanoes occur where they do, and have learnt a great deal about how they erupt. They can also explain how volcanic eruptions fit into a set of ideas called plate tectonics, which tries to explain patterns of continental movement, mountain-building and volcanic and earthquake activity. However, researchers are still trying to identify methods of accurately predicting volcanic eruptions before they occur.

▲ This vulcanologist is using a laser measuring device to monitor a bulge that is growing in the side of a volcano. The bulge indicates that magma is nearing the surface.

Early warning signs

From studying a number of eruptions in the last twenty years, scientists know that several changes take place just before a volcano erupts. They use a range of instruments to measure these changes.

• Minor earthquakes often occur as magma rises within the crust just before an eruption and forces the rocks apart. Waves of energy from the earthquakes travel through the surrounding rocks and are recorded by instruments called seismometers. By comparing seismometer recordings, scientists can pinpoint where the earthquakes are being triggered and so can work out how close the magma is getting to the surface.

• The mixture of gases in the air above the volcano may change as rising magma reaches the surface. The amounts of sulphur dioxide, carbon dioxide and hydrochloric acid in the atmosphere may increase before an eruption.

• The volcano may physically change in shape. Magma inside the mountain can cause bulging of the volcano's sides. Tiltmeters can be used to record accurately even small changes in the shape of a volcano. Measuring devices that use lasers to record tiny changes are also used.

• As it nears the surface molten magma may increase the temperature of water above and below the ground.

To measure any of these changes, scientists have to monitor volcanoes closely. The changes are often small and may not occur until just before the actual eruption. However, scientists are also able to use computer models to suggest, from past eruptions, where the most severe lava flows, mudflows and floods might be expected. They can take action to move people away from the most dangerous areas. These techniques were used most recently in Montserrat (see pages 24–5) to draw up a map of danger areas.

The ground moves as the magma rises. The tiltmeter records the movement.

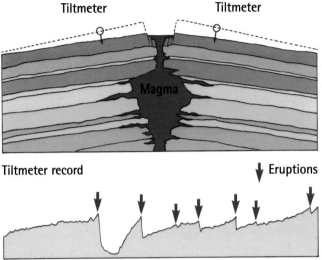

▲ Tiltmeters measure the tiny movements as magma causes the sides of a volcano to bulge outwards. The tiltmeter record shows how the bulge peaks at the time of an eruption and then goes down as the magma is released.

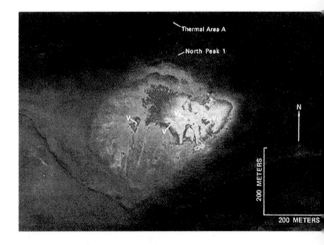

▲ This satellite image of Mount St Helens was taken about one month before it erupted in May 1980. The infra-red image shows the hottest areas of the volcano in red and the coolest in black.

Vulcanologists

Scientists who study and try to understand volcanoes are called vulcanologists. Most believe that the only way to predict precisely when a volcano is going to erupt is to study closely every new eruption that occurs.

Vulcanologists travel all over the world to examine and measure volcanoes while they are still erupting. They need to take sensible precautions against the intense heat which they will encounter. Heat-resistant, usually metal-coated, suits and asbestos gloves are worn for protection.

Through the years, many people have lost their lives around volcanoes. Those killed are often people who live nearby. Sometimes, journalists and photographers reporting on the eruption are killed. Occasionally scientists studying the volcano are killed as they carry out their dangerous work.

▲ A vulcanologist in a metal-coated protective suit with visor and gloves, in front of a lava flow at Krafla in Iceland.

LANDSBERG'S LAST FILM

Robert Landsberg was a 48-year-old photographer from Portland, Oregon, in the USA. In April and May 1980 he made dozens of visits to photograph Mount St Helens in the run-up to its eruption. On the morning of May 18, he was about 6 km from Mount St Helens, his camera mounted on its tripod, film loaded, when the mountain exploded. An ash cloud rushed towards him as he hurriedly took what turned out to be his last few frames. He managed to take one roll of film. Seventeen days later his body was found in the ash, together with the film which cost him his life.

Vulcanologists take such risks to try to prevent more lives from being lost in other eruptions. One volcano that they are monitoring very closely is Vesuvius in Italy. Vesuvius has erupted many times since AD 79. Vulcanologists are concerned that a plug of solid rock may now have formed in the vent, causing tremendous pressure to build up in the magma chamber below. There is a danger that the next eruption could be a very big one.

Below Vesuvius lies the city of Naples. Over a million people live there and in the surrounding towns and villages. Plans have been made to evacuate the area if the volcano threatens to erupt, but plenty of advance warning will be needed to move so many people. This is why constant monitoring is so vital. Vulcanologists are all too aware that, while accurate predictions can minimize the risk, nothing they can do will prevent the volcano's awesome power from being unleashed.

▼ Vesuvius: how explosive will the next eruption be?

Glossary

Active This word is used to describe a live volcano which still erupts from time to time.

Basalt A type of volcanic rock formed from thin, runny lava which flows quickly.

Caldera A steep-walled basin formed in the top of a volcano after the summit walls have collapsed inwards on to an empty magma chamber.

Cone A mass of new rock which builds up around the point at which the magma comes to the earth's surface.

Core The centre of the earth, found below the crust and the mantle. It has an outer liquid part and an inner solid part.

Crater The hole at the top of a volcano.

Crust The outer layer of the earth.

Dormant A volcano which is not currently erupting, but which could erupt again.

Eruption When magma (molten rock) and other materials rise from the mantle to reach the earth's crust.

Extrusive Describes rock that forms when lava cools on the earth's surface.

Extinct A volcano that will not erupt again.

Geothermal energy Energy found in volcanic areas that results from the natural heat of the rocks or hot springs.

Geyser A natural hot spring which shoots jets of steam and water into the air.

Hot spot A weak place in the earth's crust, some distance from the boundary of a plate, where magma rises to produce volcanoes.

Intrusive Describes rock which forms when lava cools inside the earth.

Lahar A mudflow that forms when volcanic ash is mixed with melting snow and ice or water.

Magma The molten or liquid rock in the mantle and core of the earth, melted by the extremely high temperatures there.

Mantle The thick layer of molten material found below the earth's crust.

Plate A large piece of the earth's surface made up of oceanic and continental crust.

Pumice Very lightweight rock, formed when lava cools quickly.

Pyroclastic flow A mixture of very hot ash, dust and volcanic gases which is thrown out of the volcano and moves downhill at great speed.

'Ring of Fire' The name given to the area around the Pacific Ocean where many of the world's volcanoes are found.

Tephra Airborne volcanic ash and dust.

Tsunami A large tidal wave resulting from movement of the earth's crust. It may be linked to either earthquakes or volcanic eruptions.

Vent The 'pipe' inside a volcano through which magma travels before reaching the earth's surface as a lava flow.

Volcano A vent or crack in the earth's surface through which magma, gases and ash escape or erupt. Volcano is also the name given to the landform, usually cone-shaped, which results from the material that erupts.

Vulcanologist A scientist who studies volcanoes.

Further Information

BOOKS AND ARTICLES

The Changing World: Earthquakes & Volcanoes edited by Steve Parker (Belitha, 1996)

Discoveries:Volcanoes and Earthquakes, edited by Dr Eldridge M Moores (Macdonald Young Books, 1995)

DK Pockets: Volcanoes by John Farndon (Dorling Kindersley, 1998)

Focus on Disaster: Volcano by Fred Martin (Heinemann, 1996)

Project Homework: Volcanoes by Jacqueline Dineen (Watts, 1991)

Restless Earth: Volcanoes & Earthquakes by Terry Jennings (Belitha, 1998)

Usborne Understanding Geography: Earthquakes & Volcanoes by F. Watt (Usborne, 1994)

'St Helens: Mountain with a death wish' in *National Geographical* magazine, January 1981, pp2–65. Series of articles about the 1980 Mount St Helens eruption with excellent photographs.

CD-ROMS

Violent Earth (Wayland Multimedia, 1997) PC and MAC versions available. Looks at earthquakes, floods, hurricanes, tornadoes and duststorms as well as volcanoes.

Interfact:Volcanoes (Two-Can, 1998) Book and CD-ROM (dual-platform for PC and MAC). The CD-ROM includes interactive activities, puzzles and games.

WEB SITES

The world-wide web has hundreds of volcano-related sites. Here are a few places to start:

www.disasterrelief.org/ A web site which provides up-to-date information on the latest volcanic eruptions (and other disasters). The site is run by the American Red Cross, CNN Interactive and IBM.

www.discovery.com/news/earthalert/990111/index/volcanoes.index.html This website can also give you the latest news on eruptions around the world.

www.volcano.und.nodak.edu/ Volcano World is a massive site that contains everything you could wish to know about volcanoes. It even has an 'Ask a Vulcanologist' feature, just in case you cannot find what you are looking for on the hundreds of pages which the site has to offer.

www.volcano.und.nodak.edu/vwdocs/current_volcs/montserrat/montserrat.html Try this web site for the latest information on the situation in Montserrat.

Index

Page numbers in bold refer to illustrations.